Diary Of A Pastor's Wife

How I Lost My Pastor, My Husband, My Life.

By Evangelist Gloristine Watts

Inquiries and Book Orders should be addressed to:

Great Writers Media
Email: info@greatwritersmedia.com
Phone: 877-600-5469

ISBN: 978-1-961416-41-3 (sc)
ISBN: 978-1-961416-42-0 (ebk)

Introduction

I'm a woman of faith kept by grace.

I've come through the storm but stayed in the race.

I set no other God before me; I had Jesus in my view.

Many saw me struggle, but only a few knew.

I was cast down, but not destroyed.

Sometimes perplexed, but not in despair.

For truly God saw me through.

So in this book I share with you, My Life:

The Diary Of A Pastor's Wife.

Dedication

T HIS BOOK IS DEDICATED TO GOD, MY family, friends and all the Saints that helped me. To all my children, Johnny, Vernell, Sabrina and John. To all my grandchildren, Brittney, Breana, Raquel, Quintarius, John Freeman III, and Shonda Dixions. I hope this book will be inspirational, encouraging and healing to your lives, as it has been a blessing to me writing and sharing some of my life experiences.

This book is also dedicated to every woman who wants inner peace in the midst of a storm. To the woman who just thinks she cannot make it without her husband or ex-husband, the woman who thinks no one cares about her, ***GOD DOES CARE.***

Pastor, my ex-husband was born in Macon, Georgia, July 29, 1946. There he met me, his wife Gloristine and we were married April 8, 1967. The Lord blessed us with three children, Sabrina, Johnny and Vernelle, and three grandchildren. Pastor and I were born again in 1977, where we were faithful members of Faith Temple Holiness Church in Macon, Georgia. Pastor was called by God to preach the gospel to every living creature. Pastor began his ministry on the streets of Macon, bringing souls to Christ. The Lord moved he and I to Atlanta, Georgia, September 1985. Pastor was the founding Pastor of the Church of God, Inc., on November 25, 1984.

In 1985, Pastor and I moved to Atlanta, GA to start a church in our apartment in Clarkston. The church had two members to start off with. When God started blessing us in 1988, the church moved from our apartment to the basement on Cedar Street in Scottsdale. With fifteen faithful members our crusade was moving. The Lord began to increase the membership. So, the Church of God moved to

Main Street in Stone Mountain, in 1990 where the Lord continued to bless us. Then the congregation moved with its forty-five members to 319 Aldridge Avenue and the Lord continued to bless us. Finally the congregation moved to Scottsdale, Georgia where we continue blessing God today for our Pastor and First Lady.

January 10, 1996, Pastor served me with divorce papers, and told me that he did not love me anymore. That we could no longer get along. He said, "you are supposed to live holy." He told me you can try and stop this divorce if you want to, but it will not work. I told him, "Serve it and watch me try to stop it." So we began to argue, or if you want to call it that, trying to make things right. In the back of my mind something was not right. I told him it was something deeper than what was going on right now. In fact, I knew it was not the fact that he was not getting along with me, but getting along with someone else (getting along very well with someone else). He told me that it was nothing he had done wrong, and I needed to compose myself or "get myself together."

This man wanted me to get myself together, he had just told me he no longer wanted to be with me, how was I suppose to react to such news, but his unrealistic expectation shall continue. He informed me to go to church and tell the congregation that I was sorry for accusing him of having an affair with one of the church members. I asked the ever-holy one if he had heard the old saying 'the mountain not coming to you but you coming to the mountain?' I then turned and faced my beloved and solemnly stated, "I will not do anything such as this, let them come to me, the wrong was done unto me!"

We went to Newark, Delaware on February 14, 1997, and when we returned he told me we were getting a divorce. Should I hear this once more? Should my heart be wrenched once again, or should I have held it in my heart to show him the pain. I told him if that is what he wanted then it's up to him. He said, "Well it's done" He served me with divorce papers on April 11, 1998, and our divorce was finalized November 25, 1998. He is the Pastor of our church, the husband in my life, the father of our children and most of all, an ordained minister of God and he married another woman, and the members of our church have the nerve to call him "Bishop". The

Bible states, "If a man desires the office of Bishop, he desireth a good work. A Bishop then must be blameless, the husband of one wife." (Timothy 3-1). The verse does not say two, Amen. The qualities of Bishops are to not give wine, nor strike the greedy, filthy, or lucre, but be patient, not a brawler, not covetous.

One that rules his own house, having his children under subjection with all gravity to no one else's children. For, if a man know not how to rule his own house, how shall he take care of the Church of God, which is the body of Christ.

Pastor has committed adultery; he divorced me and married again. Jesus said "Whosoever shall put away his wife, and marry another, committeth adultery against her." (Mark 10:11) If a woman should put away her husband and be married to another, she commiteth adultery. I stand on the Word of God. Jesus say unto you that, "Whosoever looketh on a woman to lust after her hath committeth adultery with her already in his heart." Jesus said in Matthew 5:32, "Unto you that whosoever put away his wife, saving for the cause of fornication, causeth her to commit adultery." Whosoever shall marry her that is divorced committeth adultery. God is good; he continuously keeps me from sin. The Holy Ghost will keep you from all sin as well.

The Word of God reads in I Corinthians 7:2, "Nevertheless to avoid fornication let every man have his own wife. Let every woman have her own husband." If they stay with their own husband and do what is right, they will not have time for another woman's husband. The husband needs to do the same also. I am talking to all women, not only Pastors' wives. It is a loss to go to church where the Pastor has been divorced or remarried. The word clearly tells us that marriage is forever; a woman is to cleave to her husband and a husband cleaves to his wife. The problem is, as men and women of Christ we do not fully understand the meaning of the word 'cleave'. My life as First Lady of the church became scandalous. Especially when both wife and mistress are members of the same church. "The wife is bound by the law as long as her husband liveth, but if he is dead, she is at liberty to be married to whom she will only in the Lord." I Corinthians 7:39.

I John 4:11 says, "If God so loved us we ought to also love one another." My husband left, and would not buy any food nor would he agree to pay for any utility bills. I Timothy 3:5 says, "For if a man know not how to rule his own house, how shall he take care of the church of God?" My gas got cut off in February of 1997. It was a blistering cold day and my mind had convinced me that it had never been this cold in my entire life. The devil must have laid down his pitchfork and traded his red tail and heels for a snowsuit and igloo and set up camp in my house, that's how cold it was. Through prayer and belief, God showed me once again that, there was no power none greater than His and our gas was shortly restored.

Many times we did not have food to eat, but God supplied our needs. Mr. Russell, a good friend of mine, came by and brought Quintarious and me food every day. When he would go fishing, he would bring us fish. We had fish and grits for dinner, supper and breakfast. I remember one day we were so hungry and did not have any food. I went down to Winn Dixie and I looked in the dumpster and got us some food. It was fried chicken, cookies and other food. I said, "Thank God for the food". It's something like, when God fed multitudes of people with fish and bread. To some it remains to be a mystery how so many people ate with so little, but to me it was a miracle such as my life.

You can not say what you will not do. I remember when I was a little girl, I use to go to the Farmers market and look in the dumpster and get peas, greens, potatoes and fruit to take home for my family to eat. The Word of God says in I Philippians 4:12, "I know both how to be abased, and I know how to abound. Everywhere and in all things I am instructed both to be full and to be hungry, both to abound and to suffer need." My husband showed me no love, but there is no love greater than the love of God. We were married 33 years, he was supposed to be saved and he let the devil destroy his home and family. I tell your wives who are having trouble in your marriages, stand still, God will fight your battle.

Pastor loved money and women more than God. The love of money is what? That's right, the root of all evil. I timothy 6:10 says, "For the love of money is the root of all evil." As a reference I have shown you what the Bible clearly states. While some covet after, they have erred from the faith and prevailed themselves through with much sorrow. Thou, Oh men of God flee these things and follow after righteousness, godliness, faith, love, patience and meekness. If a man will not provide for his family and especially for those of his own house, he hath denied the faith and that's worse than infidelity. A Bishop must be blameless as the Steward of God. Not self-willed, not soon angry, not given to wine, no striker, not given filthy, but in work they deny him being abominable and disobedient and unto every good work reprobate. I tell you stay with God. He will take care of you. God said, He will never leave you, nor forsake you. He will be there for you to the end.

September 4, 1999, Pastor married another woman.. I did not know he was dating this woman. He brought her to church on Mother's Day, May 9, 1999, and told the congregation this is his fiancé. Our daughter, Sabrina, was there and she did not like it at all. Sabrina, our daughter, got up and left and he told his members that he was going to get married whether they liked it or not. He told Sabrina that he had been dating the woman for two years and our daughter, Sabrina, told him you mean to tell me you have been seeing this woman for two years. Our daughter told him you and mom was not divorced, and you were going with this other woman while you andmom were still married. He said "But we were separated." Sabrina said, "I didn't know you can date another woman and still be married." He said we do not see one another. We just went out to eat together to get to know one another. My daughter said that's not right, you are a married man; you and mom were still married. Romans 8:5 says, "For they that are after the flesh do mind the things of the flesh; but they that are after the spirit mind the things of the spirit."

The woman that married Pastor called my house February 1997 and asked to speak to him. I told her he was not in. She told me to tell him she thanks him for speaking over Bill's funeral. She said tell him he spoke comforting words. And tell him I fell and broke my foot in two places so I want him to pray for me. When Pastor came home that night I told him she called to say thank you for the encouraging words you spoke over Bill and she wanted you to pray for her; she fell and broke her foot in two places. I told him, but he didn't respond; he turned and walked away. It was only after Pastor and she were married that I put it all together…she was right, she needed him to pray for her. John 10:10 says "The thief cometh not but to steal and to kill." Pastor let the devil come in and steal his marriage, a marriage of 33 years. Pastor always said, "I will let no one separate me from the love of God." He always said, "I would not let any woman separate me from God; spend a few minutes in lust, die and go to hell…I am not going to hell for anybody." Luke 13:3 reads, "I tell you, nay: but except ye repent, ye shall all likewise perish." I read in the Bible what Jesus taught concerning divorce. Luke 16:18, "Whosoever putteth away his wife and marries another committeth adultery and whosoever marries her that is put away from her husband, committeth adultery."

Matthew 5:31 says, "It has been said whosoever shall put away his wife, let him give her a writing of divorcement. But Jesus said unto you that whosoever shall put away his wife, saving for the cause of fornication, causeth her to commit adultery: and whosoever shall marry her that is divorced committeth adultery." I did not commit adultery, but Pastor did. He always said, "I married the best and I don't need the rest. If any woman get fresh with me, I'll just tell my wife." What happened to the best? Everything he preached about he went back on… God's Word. Like the dog eats his own vomit, he lies; he told me he would not take care of me. That no police or judge can make him support me. In fact, Sister Pam told the court that Pastor did not have any money. That the church only pays him $750. So the judge ordered him to give me $350 for three years, just because she told that lie. She also told the judge that I ran all the members away from the church. She lied and said that I told a lie on Pastor that he was dating one of the Evangelists in the church. I did not run anyone away. They left because he was not right.

I want to tell something to all you Pastor's wives who are going through things with women in the church that say they love you, but all the time they are after your husband. This woman that was in the church where my husband was Pastor, they dated for about six years, he left her and married someone else. She did me really bad about my husband and he turned around and married someone else. The Word of God says in Galatians 6:7, "For whatsoever a man soweth, that shall he also reap." What she did to me she paid for it and Pastor will get his and that woman he married will reap the consequences of their decision. God was not in Pastor's decisions or actions. The woman Pastor dated for six years left the church because he was getting married to someone other than her. My husband took me to court for a divorce. The Bible says in I Corinthians 6:1, "Dare any of you, having a matter against another, go to law before the unjust, and not before the saints? Do ye not know that the saints shall judge the world? and if the world shall be judged by you, are ye unworthy to judge the smallest matters?"

Pastor told his congregation to call him Bishop. The Word of God says in I Timothy 3:1, "This is a true saying… if a man desireth the office a Bishop then he must be blameless, the husband of one wife, (not two); one that ruleth well his own house, having his children in subjection with all gravity (meaning manages). (For if a man know not how to rule his own house, how shall he take care of the church of God?)" Pastor had a Deacon in his church to marry him on September 4, 1999. Likewise must the deacon be grave, not double tongue, but those deacons were not faithful, they went along with whatever the Pastor said whether it was right or wrong. One of the deacons was his best man. The people that left that church loved God. They were not going to stay there because it was not right for the divorce and then marriage to someone else, so they left. They will say Pastor think he's right, he always said they call right/wrong and wrong/right. That's what happen to him, a reprobate mind.

The Bible says in I John 4:15 "Whosoever shall confess that Jesus is the Son of God, God dwelleth in him and He in God, and we have known and believed the love that God hath to us. God is love and he that dwelleth in love dwelleth in God, and God in him." My husband told me he would help me, but he lied. He did not want to pay the mortgage and buy food when I was in need. He would not help me, he would help other people, like his church members.

The Word of God say all unrighteousness is sin. If a man say I love God and hateth his family or his brother, he is a liar. For he that loveth not his brother or family whom he hath seen, how can he love God whom he hath not seen? Let us love one another for love is of

God, and every one that loveth is born of God, and knoweth God. (I John 4:6.) I John 4-8 says, "He that loveth not knoweth not God; for God is love."

Pastor preached the Word of God and now he is a witness against his own self.

The Word says in I John 3:9, "Whosoever is born of God doth not commit sin; for his seed remaineth in him: and he cannot sin, because he is born of God." The seed is the Word of God. What happen to Pastor? What happen to him was this, I John 2:16,

"For all that is in the world, the lust of the flesh, and the lust of the eyes, and the pride of life, is not of the father, but is of the world. And the world passeth away, and the lust thereof; but he that doeth the will of God abideth for ever." I tried to make my marriage work, but he did not want it to work. The devil got in his mind and told him to divorce me. I tell you wives who are going through, stay with God. James 1:2 says, "Count it all joy when ye fall into divers temptations." James 1:12 says, "Blessed is the man that endureth temptation; for when he is tried, he shall receive the crown of life, which the Lord hath promised to them that love Him." Pastor just let the devil mess him up, really bad, and remember when someone wants to do wrong, it is never God. God never wants to do wrong, it is the devil. Then when lust hath conceived it brings forth sin, and sin, when it is finished, bringeth forth death. It is sad when the Pastor knows the Word of God and turns his back on His Word. 2 Peter 2:21 says "For it had been better for them not to have known the way of righteousness. Than after they have known it, to turn from the Holy Commandment delivered unto them. But it happened unto them according to the true Proverb the DOG IS TURNED TO HIS OWN VOMIT AGAIN, and the sow that was washed to her wallowing in the mire." I heard Pastor when he would say all the time at Church "follow me as I follow Christ. When you see me leave Christ, you leave me alone." And that's what some of the church members did, they left. You've got to live this Word.

Bible say in Job 20:5, "that the triumphing of the wicked is short, and the joy of the hypocrite but for a moment." God is tired of people playing church, and lying on Him. Pastor was suppose to go out of town, but he could not because the woman he married, her daughter got sick. But when our daughter was in ICU in 1998, he did not stay with her. He went on out of town with the other woman he was dating in the church. He just did not care anything about his own children since our daughter and our son was not speaking to him.

I remember when my son Johnny called me to tell me that his sister Nell was in ICU. I told Johnny I did not have any way to get up there. I figured I would call around to her house and see if Pastor was around. The Sister answered the phone. I said can I speak to Pastor, she gave the phone to her and she told me don't you call my house you old heifer. I said listen Sister, will you please listen. Nell is in ICU and I want you to tell Pastor that he needs to go up there and see what is going on. She said she would tell him but you can't be calling my house you old heifer you, he is not around here. But when Johnny got to the hospital to see how Nell was doing, Pastor and that Evangelist was there. Johnny asked her, why you call my mom a heifer. She said because she called my house and she shouldn't call my house.

Pastor has three granddaughters, but he only visits two of them. He won't visit the other one. I had to raise my sister's boy since he was 8 months old, now he's 10 and Pastor is all he knew as daddy. I don't know why, but he did not treat him right. He would always take other kids at the church places, but not his grandchildren or my nephew. He would go get that woman's little boy and take him everywhere.

Our divorce was filed November 25, 1998. He jumped up and married September 4, 1999. He was already dating this lady; he dated her and the other lady at church. We went to court on October 16-28, 1998 for the divorce and the church members that was with him in his mess came to court and all of them told lies under oath, but they will get what's coming to them…every last one of them. Pastor lie too. The Judge said you all been married for 33 years and you all have to try to work this out. Pastor said 'how can two walk together except they agree'. The Judge said, I do not know what is wrong, but whatever it is will come out in the wringer. Come to court and you bring all my dirty clothes in court. You could talk things over before coming to court. The Judge told me to let it go…leave it alone. The

Judge told us that you church people raise more hell then the people who are not in church. I was saying within myself, that's why people do not want to come to church and get saved, because they see Pastors doing what the world is doing.

I Corinthians 3:16-17 says, "Know ye not that ye are the temple of God, and that the Spirit of God dwelleth in you. If any man defile the temple of God, him shall God destroy. For the temple of God is holy, Which temple ye are." God's Word says in I Corinthians 9:13, "Do ye not know that they which minister about holy things live of the things of the temple?" You got to live what you preach. That's why people do not want to go to church. I told my daughter Nell, "Why won't you go to church on Sunday?" She said, "I do not want to go to church because those Pastors are not right. She call a church in her hometown a night club. She said the Pastor there is married, but he lust after other ladies in the church. That's why the world will not come to church because of the whoremonger Pastors who are in the pulpit.

Pastor was a man that took care of his family, but he let the devil fool him. No one wants to hear him talk about God because of what he did. The devil got him thinking he's right. He moved back to his hometown when he got married. He started a mission in his hometown. He comes up here every Wednesday-Saturday to Pastor this church. It will not work because God cannot bless you in your mess. You got to be Holy. I am living all I know how for the Lord. Pastor, you tell her what the Bible say in 2 Corinthians 6:14 "Be ye not unequally yoked together with unbelievers, for what fellowship hath righteousness with unrighteousness and what communion hath light with darkness." If you ask Pastor is that woman you are going to marry saved, he will say she love the Lord…never say she saved, because if she was saved she would never have married him, or lay up with a married man. She is not saved!

I remember one hot Saturday morning in June of '98 I did not have a car, so I walked to the store, my nephew and me. He was on his bike as I was walking down the street with 4 bags in my hand and my nephew had two on his bike; it was very, very hot that day. Pastor passed by and did not pick us up. Instead he went and called our daughter and told her I saw your Mom walking from the store.

I started to stop and pick them up, but she wouldn't want to ride. I told my daughter he could not know until he stopped. I told her he could not think for me, it was hot out there. I had to walk about five miles to work because he would not let me drive the van or the car. Pastor told me that van was for the church, not for going to work. But she (the woman he was dating) could drive it to work and keep it, but I couldn't. She would drive the car also. Pastor told me he didn't want a lot of miles on his car, but this woman he married, she could drive it to work and back everyday. When she was in an accident Pastor took her to the doctor's office two days out of every week. Would he do the same for me? No! When I was in an accident he would not take me to see the doctor.

He would get up at 6 a.m. and take her to work and to the doctor, but when I asked him to pick me up from work at 2 p.m. he just flat out said "No!" He said he was not going to stop what he was doing to pick me up. He said he had things to do. I just had to say OK and start walking five miles…it was very, very hot then. He was so dirty to me. I didn't do anything to Pastor but try to be a good wife and live Holy. I had to go to work because he would not give me any my money to get my clothes out of the laundry and to fix my hair.

Lots of times I did not have money to catch the bus. I had to walk so many miles to the store and the doctor's office. My husband was so bitter to me. I haven't done anything but just live holy. He says I argue too much, but that was not why he was dating two women. If he's holy and I am holy, why couldn't we work out our marriage? We are both saved, but he was a man who wanted everything for him self. Every time I turn around he was telling me to go. I told him I am not going anywhere. This is my house that the Lord blessed us with. He says you did not put any money down on this house. All you did was shop and bought clothes, shoes and hats, but I worked and helped out too. He was always to dressed up and looking good, but would always talk about how I dressed and wore rings on my fingers and said I came to church late wanting the people to look at me and how I was dressed. He talked about me. Had his women in the church, (her and her sister) go down to this boutique, price my clothes and come back and tell Pastor what I pay for that suit. So when I asked him to buy some food for the house, he would tell me you went and paid $300.00 for clothes, hats and shoes, you ought to buy your own food. He said it's not his responsibility to take care of Quintarius and me. You get that boy's check. He also said if we would leave, he could rent that room out, because he needs the money.

I had clothes to buy for him and pay some bills. That money was just a small amount. Out of that money I would buy his clothes and give Pastor $160.00 on mortgage every month. He was blessed with enough money to pay the mortgage, but I had to give him some of this money when the check came for Quintarius. He just wanted me to leave so he could bring that woman in this house, but I did not leave the house that God Bless us with. God is good to me. What the devil meant for my bad, God meant for my good. What God had for me, it was for me.

I went to the doctor and they told me that I had Sleep Disorders. I told Pastor, my ex-husband, what the Doctor said; it's call Sleep Apnea. So I have to have an oxygen system before I fall asleep; the air pressure helps oxygen get to my lungs. Without the oxygen system the doctor says I could die in my sleep because of high blood pressure. I told Pastor what the doctor said about the system costing $300.00 and he said I do not have that kind of money to pay for an oxygen system and so he did not get it. But my God made away and I got it anyway. Thank God!

I went through something, but God brought me through like I knew he would. You wives stay with God, he will take care of you. My husband just wants to be boss, and run everybody's life. I did let him boss me around like a child. I know the Word of God say in Ephesians 5:22, "Wives submit yourselves unto your own husband as unto the Lord." It did not say be a slave unto your husband, and obey him in the Lord. For the husband is the head of the wife. It does not mean treat her bad. The Word of God is true and not a lie. God cannot lie.

One day Sister Pam went to court with Pastor, that's his secretary. I needed a car to drive and Pastor had bought an '85 Buick in his name. The Church did not buy that' 85 Buick, so the judge told Pastor to give me the Buick, but to fix it up right. He did not do it, he lied.

Sister Pam and Pastor came to court and told the judge he had fixed the car, but he lied. The judge told Pastor to give me $200.00 to get to the doctor until he gets the car right. When he had patched it up he gave it back to me and it stopped running right away. I was without a car again. When we went back to court, the judge gave Pastor the Van and the Cadillac because they were in the church's name. So here I was with nothing to drive in. The members were glad I did not get the Van and Pastor was glad I did not get the Cadillac.

Ecclesiastes 9:9 says, "Live joyfully with the wife whom thou lovest all thy days of the life of my vanity. Which he hath given thee under the sun. All the days of thy vanity for that is thy portion in this life and in the labor. Which thou tastest under the sun. Whatsoever thy hand findeth to do, do it with thy might; for there is no work, nor love nor talk, nor device, nor knowledge, nor wisdom in the grave, where thou goest, there." That's why you got to treat everybody right, because you do not know where death is. Time is round up. Pastor knows he is wrong, but Oh he thinks it is okay what he did. He did not want his daughter at their wedding, because the woman he married say she did not feel comfortable with his young daughter around, so she did not go to his wedding.

Her daddy makes excuse about how she would come over to the church dressed. They had two people at the door of the wedding thinking my daughter and I would come over and so they had someone out at the telephone to call the police if we come near. Thank my God for another day He has made. I was not thinking about the devil and his games. One day I went over to the church to talk with Pastor about the house. "What are you going to do?" He said, "I am going to sell it." I told him he could not sell the house until we go back to court. He said it was his house and he could sell it if he wants to, and so we start exchanging words. He told me to leave the church and if I did not go he will call the police.

I picked up the phone and told him to call the police, I didn't care. He called them. When this policewoman came to the church he told her that he did not want me at the church because when I come I cause trouble. I told the police that he was a lie, I just wanted to talk to him about our house. He asked the police what he could do to keep me from coming over there and she told him that he would have to take a warrant out against me.

The policewoman said, "I never seen such a thing. The Pastor and the First Lady arguing about things in the church house." I just wanted my communion table and other things I bought. I wanted them because I was very, very upset with Pastor and the way he treated me, but that's all right because he will get his one day.

Ecclesiastes 3:14 "I know that whatsoever God doeth it shall be forever, nothing can be put to it, nor anything taken from it." God is not in that mess. That's the work of the devil. Pastor was an honorable man until he did all that mess and stuff. Soon as God start Blessing, he let the devil start messing. He suppose to be a strong man in the Lord, but lust got in his mind. I would never thought he would leave me and marry someone else. He said he would always love me, and down through the years he said he did not love me anymore, and I did not know why until he married again. I told him I know you love me, he said no I don't. I said yes you do. He said no I don't. He told me one day I will not need you anymore. I am going to find someone who will submit to me and obey. I told him you must have another woman, he said no, but he lied.

I remember in '96 we went to Lima, Ohio and he asked me a question about how many men have I had sex with. I told him three men and he said did you have sex with Bay when we went to Ohio years ago. I said no. I asked him how many ladies you had sex with, he started to smile. I told him I could count myself. He told me one woman movement was about like mine. I say who. He said I am not going to tell you that. I see who it was the woman he married, I guess that's who it was. I took a lot of mess off of him about his whoremongers and adulterers. I read in God's Word, Hebrew 13:4 that "marriage is honourable in all and the bed undefiled, but whoremongers and adulterers God will judge." God gave me a discerning spirit, I knew when my husband was with another woman. I John 2:20-22, "But ye have unction from the Holy One and ye know all things. I have not written unto you because ye known not the truth, but because ye know it and that no lie is of the truth."

I tried very hard to make my marriage work. He just didn't want to because he was messing around, staying with that woman before he married her. Say he is a Bishop…play with God. I stand on God's Word everything else go down but the Word of God. Jeremiah 7:3, "Amend your ways and your doings and I will cause you to dwell in this place. You can go to hell, trust ye in lying Word. Behold he trust in lying words that cannot profit." Jeremiah 7:9, "Will ye steal murder and commit adultery and swear falsely and burn incense unto Ba-al and walk after other gods whom ye know not and come and stand before me in this church which is called by my name and say we are delivered to do all these abominations?"

That's why the Pastor goes out doing everything under the sun, and come to church Sunday and preach on committing adultery after just coming from laying up with someone's wife. I do not trust any man. I put my trust in God. Man will leave you, but God will not leave you alone. He will be there until the end. My husband walked out and left me. But God did not. My husband did not want anything to do with me and I have not done anything to him, but tried to live holy and be a wife. No, I am not in agreement to his wrongdoings and his walk living for God. If anyone goes alone with him, he's fine. But if you do not go alone with him he does not want any part of you around. It hurt me the way he treats me.

If you say that you a saved Pastor, you should know how to love your wife and family. Ephesians 5:25 says, "Husbands love your wives even as Christ also loved the Church." All he cares about is them church folks, everyday and every night. Pastor will go over to the church, leave about 10:00 or 12 noon and stay gone all day. I will call to the church and he will not be there and the spirit let me know something is wrong. My daughter told me she heard that the Evangelist like daddy. I told her I did not believe that. I told my husband what was said. I told him I did not believe that the Evangelist liked him.

He went to church that Wednesday and told the church members I said someone said that he likes Evangelist and he told the church members that I do not believe that, but it was true. My daughter and the woman Pastor was going with got into a fight inside the church about her smart mouth. I called over to the church to speak to Pastor.

The woman he was going with said Pastor does not live here anymore and hung up the phone in my face. I told my daughter and she say she will ask about it Sunday when I go to church.

And she asked her and they begin to exchange words and start fighting. My daughter told her it was wrong to hang up the phone in Mom's face. If Pastor wants you all to call him Bishop that's fine, but Mom calls him by his name, that is his name. But Pastor and Mom will always communion because of the grandchildren and his children that's what my daughter told her.

It was told to me if anyone calls over to the church and does not ask to speak to Pastor but call him by his name, do not call him to the phone. She knew who I was and was just being smart. God's people do not act like that; she was always smart about anything that was said about her Pastor, which was my husband. The Bible says in I Corinthians 7:2, "Nevertheless to avoid fornication, let every man have his own wife and let every woman have her own husband." She acts like that was her husband. She cooks for him, wash and sew his clothes, and shop for him. Every place Pastor went she was there with him.

I remember one day my son and I was coming from church and he said, "Mom, there's your husband and that woman in that truck." I said, "I am going to follow them", and I did. They stopped some place to pick up one of their members. When he stopped the truck I went up to him and said, "I heard you go with her" and I start hitting him with my umbrella. He said, "What's wrong with you? Have you lost your mind?" I said, "I am going to hit her with it." He blew his horn and she jumped in the truck and told me to go home. I said, "I heard you go with my husband!" Pastor went and took a warrant out on me.

Evangelist and Pastor had an American Express Card in their name with the Church on it. They would go shopping together and to the Economy Inns and lay up. One day Pastor came home to see his newborn granddaughter, they were staying with me. Pastor came in the house, he was staying at the church at the time. He told Nell, our daughter, I'll see you and he didn't speak to me at all. When he left, I went out behind him and I looked down on the ground and there was his card with her name and the Church name on it.

Pastor also had one with the Church name on it. They were having fun together and the church didn't know what they were doing with those cards. Sister Pam did, because she was the church secretary and that was her Aunt.

I went to court, and he had his members there, the Evangelist, her sister and one of the deacons. The Judge gave me 3 months probation. He told the Judge I was always following him and wanting to fight. He told him he was taking the Evangelist with him to pick up one of the members and I started to hit him with my umbrella and followed close behind him. When it was over they laughed and gave each other a high-five when the Judge gave me 3 months probation. They did me really bad, but that's all right, God kept me through it all. I just thank God for keeping me.

Pastor go around talking about God gave him a wife. He talking about the woman he married. How will God give him a wife and he already has a wife. Told people that God told him that's his wife and I know he was a lie, because he was really confused. Devil got him thinking he right, but he is wrong and do not understand what is happening to him. I hope that he will get it right.

This woman Pastor use to date about 30 years ago, she came back to the church. I met her at the doctor's office. She and I were glad to see one another. She asked me how is Pastor doing and I said we are getting a divorce. She said "No!" She said, "What happen?" I begin telling her and she said, "No way I will come back to that church." But she lied, she came back and tried to get back with Pastor, but he did not want her, he was busy messing around with the other woman. She started cooking food to bring out to the church for her Pastor, but the other woman did not like it. She also went out of town with Pastor.

She called my house and told me why are you calling up North telling them I was hanging around the church trying to get your husband. She told me I do not want your leftovers. Other words, he was my boyfriend before he was your husband. She said she came back to the church to help Pastor with the choir. She knew all the time what she was doing, trying to get back with Pastor, but he did not want her. She didn't have any money to give him like the other woman did. The woman he married gave him a check for $200.00, it bounced. One day I was looking at all the cancelled checks and I saw that the woman he married gave him a check for $200.00 in 1997. I told Pastor that the check she sent him bounced. He did not say a word. But one day at church he told the members that he went home and a lady blessed him with a check for $200.00 and I put two-and-two together. That's the same woman he married. The same woman who called my house and asked me to ask Pastor to pray for her when she broke her foot.

I am glad I stand on God's Word. He said in 2 Corinthians 5:17 "Therefore if any man be in Christ, he is a new creature. Old things are passed away, behold, all things are become new." When you are a new creature in Christ you do not do the things you use to do. You change your walk, your talk, your old way of living. You cannot be a new creature in Christ and living all kinds of ways. I myself stand on God's Word. I do not hate anybody; I love, because God is love.

God has been good to me. I learned how to trust in God. Because he made the difference in my life. Ephesians 5:28 said, "So ought men to love their wives as their own bodies. He that loveth his wife loveth himself. For no man ever yet hated his own flesh; but nourisheth and cherisheth it, even as the Lord the Church." Ephesians 5:33 says, "Nevertheless let everyone of you in particular so love his wife even as himself: and the wife sees that she reverence her husband." But my husband did not honor me. He honored every woman he was dating in the church and the women did not respect me because he did not. They would actually pick at me and call me names like, red or bald headed in front of the children so that the children would laugh at me. Both of the Evangelist would call me names and one of their sisters wanted to fight me, but I did not say anything but have a Happy New Years; that's when he took out a warrant on me.

I told Pastor what the Evangelist said to me and he said if you respect yourself then other people will. I just listen to him and did not say a word. When the Evangelist daughter told her about it her son-in-law had to pull her from my car. She was telling me to get out and what she was going to do to me. I just looked at her; I wasn't scared of her. I was not going to fight on the Church grounds anymore. The last time I pulled my shoe off and hit Pastor one night after Bible Study about that woman.

My husband, he did not stay at home, he stayed at the church all the time. He was telling me he was praying and fasting all the time. When he left home, he would not come back until late that night. I would have finished my dinner and when he came home I asked him do you want to eat and he say "No". I did my part that I had to do as a Pastor's wife. I learn to stay close to God and he will fight your battle for you. God was on my side when the devil try to beat me down, but it did not work. I am still standing tall in God's Word, I am holding on. Never give up. God is there for me. Pastor just will not stop his mess, he was right, he will not listen to any one, and he just thinks he is right all the time. God loves me because he saw my need. He said, he will supply my every need in Christ Jesus.

The Word of God say in Jeremiah 25:1 "WOE be unto the Pastors that destroy and scatter the sheep of my pasture! Saith the LORD. The Pastors that feed my people, ye have scattered my flock, and driven them away and have not visited them." When I was hungry and needed food, Pastor did not come and see about me and, the church members did not come either, nor did they call to see how I was getting along, and say that they loved me. When Pastor left me, the church members did the same.

Jeremiah 25:10 the Word of God saith for the land is full of adulterers; for because of swearing the land mourneth. Jeremiah 23:23 says, "Am I a God at hand, saith the Lord, and not a God a far off." I am glad He is not afar off. Because when I was in need for money to catch up my mortgage payment after Pastor left me, I prayed to God and he told me you have not because you ask not. So I began to ask the Saints, not the church people, and they helped me keep my house, and so did some of my friends. Jeremiah 3:24 "Can any hide himself in secret places that I shall not see himself, saith the LORD."

God let you all know whatever you do you cannot hide in secret places. He see you all, when ever you lay up in motels with that woman and that man, which is not your husband or wife, and leave at night to stay with that woman you are not married to.

God sees you when you hide late at night to that woman's house and come back to church and say God say this and God say that and lie on God. God say in His Word Jeremiah 23:31 "Behold, I am against the Pastor or prophets saith the Lord that use their tongues and say He saith." Jeremiah 23:40 says, "The Word of God saith and I will bring an everlasting reproach upon you and a perpetual shame, which shall not be forgotten." God is getting tired of the Pastors lying on Him. What the Pastor need to do is Wait On God, he will supply your every need.

The Lord say I will bring upon that land all my Words which I have pronounced against it even all that is written in this book. Jeremiah 25:13 says God is good to me. I love the Lord with all my heart and soul.

Pastor is going around telling people he is buying a big house with a swimming pool. When we were together he did not want a house with a swimming pool. He always say the grandchildren will come over to play and we might not be looking out for them and they will get in the pool and drown, but all of a sudden he jumps up and buys a house with this woman and puts in a pool. Lots of things he did…he lied. He just thinks that now he got it going on. When we were together, he did not want me to hang pictures on the wall. Said he didn't want any holes in his walls, everything is my, my, my… never ours.

For what is a man profit if he shall gain the whole world and lose his own soul. Or what shall a man give in exchange for his soul. Walk with God. You cannot kill one sin with another, you have to repent to God, and he will forgive you of your sins. Romans 8:1 says, "There is therefore no condemnation to them which are in Christ Jesus who walk not after the flesh, but after the Spirit. For if ye live after the Flesh ye shall die, but if ye through the Spirit do mortify the deeds of the body ye shall live." I always will. Pastor say examine yourself, but he did not examine himself, see what happen to him.

I believe in the Word of God…strong. 2 Corinthians 5:17 says, "Therefore if any man be in Christ, he is a new Creature old things are passed away, behold, all things are become new." God cannot lie, when you are born again God has changed you. You do not do the things you use to do, for you are a new creature. For godly sorrow worketh repentance to salvation not to be repented nor to the sorrow of the world worketh death. I always will hear Pastor say "Be ye not unequally yoked together with unbelievers, For what fellowship hath righteousness with unrighteousness and what communion hath light with darkness? And what agreement hath the temple of God with idols."

I remember I saw Pastor and the woman he married. I spoke with him and the people in the van and they did not speak. He act like he was scared to speak to me. I went home to my friend's funeral. I stayed with my daughter, Nell. One morning Pastor came over. My granddaughter, Chocolate said, "Mom, its Granddaddy." She opened the door and he came in. When he saw me sitting at the kitchen table he could have went through the floor. He looked at me and said, "Oh, I didn't know she was here." Then he talked with our granddaughter for awhile and then he left. He told Nell he would see her later. I said, "Pastor, you can't speak?" He looked at me and went right out the door and still did not say a word. My granddaughter said, "What's wrong with Granddaddy?" I said, "He needs prayer, for he is sick. Suppose to be a man of God, but he will not speak; just pray for him."

He has 3 grandchildren and do not call or come to see them… something is wrong with that. He always says I love my grandchildren and will do what I can to help them, but he lied. I will not let no woman or man come against my grandkids, but that's what he did. He told me that woman respects him, like I did. He has a very serious problem, what he want me to do, I really don't understand. If she respects him and is good to him that's his business. I did my part for 33 years of marriage and he will pay for what he did. It is with him and God. I do not have a problem speaking to him and her. He got the problem, not me, because it is over.

I am an Evangelist and I am writing this book to all Pastors' wives that are going through. I did not get a chance to talk with Pastor about anything or the church members because everyone was on his side. They did not listen to me. They would listen to everything Pastor said about me, but that's all right, God has everything in control.

On March of 2000 our oldest granddaughter asked me "Mom, can I call Daddy". I say, "Of course." When she start to dial the number I walked out of the room, but as I turned the corner I heard her on the speaker phone say, "Daddy can you give me $20.00". He did not respond to her about the money, he asked Precious "Where is Breana?" She said, "Right here." Her granddaddy said in a tone of voice "Breana why did you call over here and leave that hot message?" She said, "Daddy I do not know." He said, "Listen to me, you never do that again, you do not do that. I am not anyone to play with. Who told you to say that?" She said, "Nobody." He said, "Let me speak to Precious." He asked her, "Who told you to call over here?" She said, "Breana." He told her you do not do what Breana say. You know right from wrong and told her I talk with you later.

I came in the room and I asked Breana what did you say when you call over there. She replied, I told him you do not have time for us, all you have time for is your fake wife and your other grandchildren. I asked, "Breana, when did you call over there?" She said, "Saturday." I did not know she called over there. He thinks I pushed her up to do that, but I did not. Proverbs 20:11 says, "Even a child is known by his doings, whether his work be pure and whether it be right." The grandchildren know right from wrong, they know their granddaddy do not come and see them or call. They talk about it all the time. I tell them your Uncle Johnny will be home soon and he will spend time with you all and take you places.

If their granddaddy love them like he says, he does, he would call or come to see them. Love is action, not talk. I John 3:18 says, "My little children, let us not love in Word, neither in Tongue, but in deed and in truth, that we should love one another." I would not let anyone separate me from my family. He always would say that I love my grandchildren, but love is action. He will not return their calls. He always says no one will stop me from giving to my grandchildren. I am always going to do for them, but he doesn't do for Breana, but he buys and gives Precious the oldest grandchild. He always will tell me he did not believe that Sabrina was his daughter. I did no wrong about that, the devil is a liar. From the beginning and abode not in the truth, because there is no truth in him. When he speaketh a lie, he speaketh of his own; that's the Word of God, not my word… God Word. Every since Breana daddy passed away he hasn't done anything for her and says he loves her. I know God is love, all that I went through. I heard Job says in 13:15 "Though He slay me, yet will I trust in him, but I will maintain mine own ways before him."

I trust in God for all my needs. Man will fail you, but God will not. God is not slack in His Word. He promised to take care of me if I live Holy. I heard Job say in 15:14 "What is man that he should be clean? And he which is born of a woman, that he should be righteous." Job 15:16 says, "How much more abominable and filthy is man, which drinketh iniquity like water." God hates sins, but he loves us, because He died for our sins that we might live right.

March of 2000 his grandchildren call over to the church to ask him for money, he did not return their call. The woman he married does not want him to have anything to do with his grandkids. He promised me he was going to help me out with my bills. He lied. He told me that he would do anything to help me. Our granddaughter, Breana, call to the church and told her granddaddy "You do not take up time with us anymore for being with that fake wife and them other grandchildren." He thinks I told her to say that, I did not. They are smart children. They know that their granddaddy do not call or come and see them. I told them to leave him alone; he knows what's right or wrong. When he left me in '97 he did not want to buy me a stove. I have been cooking on a hot plate for 6 years or more, but he gets married, fixes up and paints another house for the woman he married and he says he loves God? And God is love. Where is the love? Love is action, not talk! He could not fix the house we live in. That's not right!

I even got to the point where I was willing to forgive this man for adultery, even though some of his affairs were with women I called Sister in the Lord. I was willing to forgive him for adultery and abuse as long as he was there for me. It was as if my whole life was Hell. He wanted to control me. He wanted me to be his child. I told him I was not a child, I'm a grown woman. After 32 years of fighting with satan I learned you have to leave it to God. I could not do it by myself. I learned each day of my life that I have to let go and do not let satan be my stumbling block. I had to learn that you must love God and yourself before you can love someone else. I had to learn that the most important thing I have in this life is my relationship with God. Nothing else matters to me more than my relationship with God. Only God can help us with the different issues we face today.

I learned while I was going through my trials; we will never be disappointed as long as we have Jesus Christ on our side. Psalm 124 says, "If it had not been the Lord who was on our side."

I had to ask God to help me to overcome that horrible relationship I had with my husband. God has taught me to trust in him not in man. It is God's love and mercy that keeps me each day. For 32 years I listened to my ex-husband tell me you do not have anything. You got nothing. I told him I got Jesus that's enough for me. He would call me stupid and fat. He would tell me I needed to wear lipstick and makeup sometimes. I need to get a wig because my hair had come out bad because of what he took me through. I know God loves me. The Bible tells me in John 3:16 that, "God so loved the World that He gave His only begotten Son, that whosoever believeth in Him should not perish, but have everlasting life."

When I was married to Pastor, my ex-husband, somedays I felt like he did not love me anymore because of the other women he was around all the time. Since he divorced me, everyday I wake up and I feel good about myself. Thank God for waking me up and clothing me in my right mind. I have my health and strength and my children and grand-children are still alive. I might not have any money, but I got JESUS.

Pastor, my ex-husband always would talk about love, but charity begins at home. He would love the people who take care of his needs and love the people who are there when he need something, as long as they give him money and buy him suits, he loves them. But what about his family? When we are children our love is based on feelings. He always say that feelings will change. He carried that attitude of love into his adult life. He only loves the people who are doing something for him. That will benefit him. He fails to understand the true meaning of unconditional love. He fails to understand that love is a principle as well as an emotion. We should love people for who they are and not for what they can do for us. Then we will fully understand what true love is all about.

God created us to love one another, not out of feelings. I use to tell Pastor, my ex-husband; you do not love me. He would say I do not. How can he love God and never see Him and do not love his family. He must first love God, and then himself…then he can love his family. Then he can love unconditionally. God created us out of love, not out of feelings. He is love!

God is love and is a good friend when you need one. Love is like glue that keeps a marriage together. True love can be whatever you want it to be when you truly love God and your family and understand the real meaning of God's Love. I Corinthians 13:1 says, "Though I speak with the tongues of men and of angels and have not charity..I am nothing." When Pastor, my ex-husband, left me in 1997, I went through storms raging in my life, but I did not give up. A winner does not give up. When storms rage I look at what I came out of, not what I was going through. I keep my eye on the Lord's Word. He said he would never leave me, nor forsake me. God has been good to me while I was going through the storms a-raging in my life.

God was there for me all the time. Pastor, my ex-husband will tell me I don't love you or want you. Then I would tell him to leave and he would say you leave, this is my house. My name was not on the mortgage. He would tell me he was going to sell the house, so I was between a rock and a hard place. I did not want to move back home. I just had to pray and wait for God to work things out for me, and He did.

After the divorce we went to court and I got the house. I went through very bad verbal abuse. He would not buy me food, would not take me to the store or buy my blood pressure medicine. He did not pay the mortgage for one year. He left and moved into the church. He did not have to pay any bills. All my bills got behind. He would not help me at all and talk about he is a man of God. Where is the love? I need God to help me. The Word says in Jeremiah 33:3, "Call to me and I will answer you and will shew you great and hidden things which you have not known."

I started to pray and call upon God for help, strength and guidance. I had to stop being dependent on Pastor, my ex-husband for my happiness and my needs. I had to totally rely on God for all my human needs. Philippians 4:19 says, "My God will supply every need of yours according to His riches in glory in Christ Jesus."

A lot of times I would look for a good time to pray, but there was not special time for me to pray and talk to my God. I talked to God as I would to my best friend. He is my best friend. Proverbs 18:24 says, "And there is a friend that sticketh closer than a brother." We have to remember that satan is on the job every day and night, second and minute; we just have to keep on praying if we want victory over satan through Jesus. I know it was very hard for me to pray with the attitude I had for those church people. What they took me through. I am the first one to admit that. I just had to practice each day in putting God first in all of my affairs and have faith that He will work everything out for me and for my best.

I remember that God loves me in the midst of my storm, He is there for me. We all have some type of storm that we go through everyday. My storm I went through was a stormy divorce. I was married for 32 years when he decided to put me away and marry someone else, but I stayed with God through all my trials. The Bible says in Isaiah 54:17 "No weapon that is formed against thee shall prosper, and every tongue shall rise against me in judgment thou shalt condemn. This is the heritage of the servants of the Lord, and their righteousness is of me saith the Lord."

I found in every life some rain and storm shall come, but I do not have to stay out there and get wet. Jesus says we are going to have trials and tribulations, but we shall overcome. But I do not have to let my trials get me off focus from my God.

April 14, 2001, I was sitting in my room thinking about my electricity being going cut off and it's just like when your electrical equipment or your lights are off you have no power source to operate them. That's what happens when I stop praying or do not pray at all; I have no access to divine power, which is the Holy Ghost. When you stop praying you play right into satan's games and he loves that. But I always pray and talk to God, morning, day and night. Prayer is my weapon through Jesus Christ against satan's attacks. I pray during the night when I am unable to sleep. Prayer is my armor against the power of darkness. Prayer is my key in all my tough situations.

I had to pray to God to help me, because the devil was so mad with me since I stand on God's Word everyday and night. They wanted to beat me down and take everything from me, but it did not work because God had my back. What God had for me it was for me.

They try to sell my house while I was living in it. No weapon they form will prosper against me, God said it. I always had faith in God. I put my faith to work and God moved for me each time. He may not come when I want Him to, but He is right on time. The just shall live by faith, not by sight. Having faith is like getting a check in the mail when you do not know where you next meal is coming from. I always keep my faith account current. I would never know when I had to make a withdrawal from God's faith account. I live by faith everyday. God has been good to me. I love the Lord, because He first loved me. I thank God for helping me while I was going through the storm of my life. So many nights I would cry thinking about what happen to me. But God knew that I would be able to bare it as long as I stayed with Him. The Bible says in Isaiah 43:2, "When thou passest through the waters I will be with thee and through the rivers, they shall not overflow thee when thou walkest through the fire. Thou shalt not be burned, neither shall the flame kindle upon thee for I am the Lord thy God."

Seven years ago, after going through many bad experiences, I wanted to move back to my hometown to be with my family. I had gone through so much that I felt the only way I could be happy was for me to go back home to Macon to be around family. I knew my family really loved me and cared, but in the meantime I was praying and asking God what to do. So God in His infinite wisdom wants me to stay in Atlanta, because He has a work for me to do here. Wherever I could be of service to Him I want to do what God say.

Going through my divorce, we all need someone to believe in us, in addition to a friend providing closeness and warmth. True friends will be there for us in our moments of weakness as well as our best days. I need a genuine friend who is there because of concern, not for the purpose of gossip about one another. I need a friend who can look me straight in the eye and tell me the truth about myself, even if the truth hurts, and be honest about everything. I need a friend to help me and encourage me to reach for the top and give me suggestions on how to get there. Thank God for all my friends that were there for me.

The types of abuse Pastor, my ex-husband took me through was physical, verbal and mental. Pastor started physically abusing me in '94 when he was dating that woman in church. He verbally abused me by calling me every name in the curse book and then some. It was like he would cut my heart into little pieces. He just did not care about how I felt. He just cared about his self and the members of his church.

Mentally would be when Pastor, my ex-husband went for weeks and months without showing me any affection. He would make love to me only when he felt the need. I know he was messing around with other women. He would say what makes you think I want you? I do not want you; it is over with you and me. Then I would tell him to leave. He would say, "I am." Then he would turn around and say "You leave, this is my house!" I know I did not put my name on the mortgage, but I know this is my house too. God blessed us with it.

I called unto the Lord. The Lord teaches us in His Word to "Call to Me and I will answer you, and will shew you great and hidden things which you have not known", Jeremiah 33. I started calling upon God for help, strength and guidance. I had to let go of being co-dependent on Pastor, my ex-husband for anything and believe in the Word of God. He said he would supply my every need.

Pastor, my ex-husband, came over to my house March 24, 2000 to see the grandchildren. I told him to come see me when he get through talking with the kids. I told Pastor I had a friend. I told him you remember when you told me that it is the devil. I told him now I have a friend. He said just be careful because men will say you look good, you fine and all that just to be next to you. He told me do not let him in the house and especially your bedroom. Once you do that he knows that he has you. When he comes to see you do not let him in your house, get to know him first. Let him come to the door. Pastor told me he was glad I had a friend. He told me to go on with my life. I was free and didn't have no one to hold me back. Pastor told me he was praying that I get someone and now I have a friend, he was lying. He did not like it, because he called me and told me to be careful out there, like I was running around in the world like he was doing. He told me disease was out there, but he married another woman.

On September 10, 2001 I called over to the church to speak to Pastor. I told him I did not get my check. He said it was not his fault the check got lost and he said I am not giving you another check. He also said he could give me that check when he is ready; before the month is out. The woman he married told me I am not getting any check. She said that she will call Social Security and tell them I was getting more money and hung up the phone in my face. I called back, but they had put the answering machine on, so I left a message telling them what was wrong and what was right.

I told Nell about it and she called Pastor and asked him why did she tell Mom that. He said she was wrong and she will not do that. Nell let him know that she had no business doing that. That's how Mom pays her bills. Pastor told Nell that he would not let her do anything like that. I called Pastor and told him I still did not receive my check. He told me that his wife mailed it yesterday and I would get it. Yesterday was a holiday and you will get it because I send you a check every month, so stop calling me about that check. He talked very cold and hung up the phone in my face. I told my daughter Nell to call him about my check that I did not get. She called him but he did not return her call. I said then page him, but she said I am not getting in the middle of your mess. Pastor asked me to stop calling him about that check.

Pastor says he put the check in the mail and he did not want me calling him because he is married and his wife is jealous. I told him she just think you want me and that I want you. She doesn't have to worry about me because you did what you want. We should all be friends because of your children and grandchildren. He said my children are grown now. I told him they are still your children and we will always have to come together because of the family, especially in sickness and in death. He just looked at me, he knew I was telling the truth.

I remember when we were in court the judge asks me if I forgive him and I said, "Yes." I thought about what Jesus said in Mark 11:24-26, "Therefore I say unto you what things soever ye desire when ye pray believe that ye receive them and ye shall have them. And when ye stand praying forgive, If ye have ought against any, that your Father also which is in heaven may forgive you your trespasses. But if ye do not forgive, neither will your Father which is in heaven forgive your trespasses."

I remember one day Pastor, Evangelist and I were going out of town. The Evangelist and her husband were getting back together. He had been gone for a long time and he was on drugs really bad. The Lord laid it on my heart to tell the Evangelist before she has sex with her husband she should wait until he takes a aids test, because you know his problem and he could have a disease. She said that's what Pastor told her to do also, to wait until he gets tested before you have sex with him. Pastor did not have any business at all telling the Evangelist that about her husband. It was my job to talk to the ladies at the church. I found out that Pastor was just trying to protect his own self, because they were dating. I remember one day he took me to Grady Hospital, I went over the church and parked my car and got in his car. I was going to put my key in the glove compartment and he knocked my hand down so hard and told me you do not go through my private stuff. I begin to think why he did not want me in his glove compartment. Now I know why! The Lord revealed to me he has condoms in his glove compartment and I told him that the Lord revealed that to me and he said I was lying on God. But the word of God says in I Corinthian 2:10, "But God hath revealed them unto us by His Spirit For His Spirit searcheth all things, yea, the deep thing of God." Titus 1:2 says, "God that cannot lie promised before the world began."

Jesus' response to the Pharisees question about divorce, Matthew 19:11 says, "But Jesus say unto them all men cannot receive this saying save they to whom it is given. For there are some eunuch's which were born from their mother's womb and there are some eunuchs were made of men; and there be eunuchs for the Kingdom of Heaven's sake. He that is able to receive it let him receive it." Pastor told his members

God told him to be a eunuch and I told him God did not tell you that. The members believe him, but I know what the Word of God said, that a Christian should not divorce, and cannot remarry.

For in true holiness, marriage is designed by God to be a covenant between two persons. If so, then the success of a marriage is never simply a question of whether the wife pleases her husband, precisely, because it takes two to make a marriage work. It is a covenant, therefore, it depends upon both parties. I found out a successful marriage is not just one in which the wife pleases the husband, but one in which both please each other. But Pastor wants to please other women. He married another woman.

Pastor and I had not been divorced but 1 year and 2 months before he married again. He told everyone at the church he is going to get married September 4, 1999. He was not going to stay single, and if the church members don't like it, they can leave. He was going to be married. He did not care who liked it or not. It is his life and he has to answer to God. That is true. The Word of God says in Galatians 6:7 "Be not deceived; God is not mocked: For whatsoever a man soweth, that shall he also reap."

This book is for my life and your life, especially for women who have had a difficult life with relationships, and mental or physical abuse. I know what I am talking about, because I have been through the storm in my life. Stand up and be a good woman. I am sharing a lot of the struggles I have been through, but my God has brought me out.

This book is from my heart and I hope that it will encourage all women who are in or have been in an abusive situation to look back on their life and say, "I am not alone. For God is with me. He says He will never leave me. ***GOD IS LOVE.***"

About the Author

MY NAME IS EVANGELIST GLORSITINE WATTS. I was born October 12, 1948 to the parents of Mr. Johnny Johnson and Mrs. Laura Ann Freeman. I have four children. I am a grandmother, I love to cook and entertain people. I love helping people. I love God and going to church… I believe God put me here on this earth to help others and to tell the story of my struggles so I can help others through their struggles. God delivered me and he can do the same for you. He will give you understanding. Love peace, joy and most of all, understanding.